WITHDRAWN

EASY & ELEGANT
HOME
DECORATING

EASY & ELEGANT
HOME
DECORATING

ANDREA MAFLIN

25 STYLISH PROJECTS FOR YOUR HOME

Facts On File, Inc.

For the most important woman in my life, my mum, Margaret Maflin. For that child in you that you have never lost; your endless sunshine, your love and constant encouragement and your proud belief in me and all I want to do.

Easy & Elegant Home Decorating:
25 Stylish Projects for Your Home

First published in Great Britain in 1998
by Collins & Brown Limited

Library of Congress Cataloging-in-Publication Data
Maflin, Andrea.
    Easy & elegant home decorating: 25 stylish projects for
    your home/Andrea Maflin.
        p. cm.
    Includes index.
    ISBN 0-8160-3829-5
    1. Handicraft. 2. House furnishings. 3. Interior decoration.
I. Title.
TT157.M342 1998
745.5–dc21   98-9360

Facts On File books are available at special discounts when purchased in bulk quantities for businesses, associations, institutions or sales promotions. Please call our Special Sales Department in New York at (212) 967-8800 or (800) 322-8755

You can find Facts On File on the World Wide Web at http://www.factsonfile.com

Design: Janet James
Photography: Lucinda Symons

Reproduction by Classic Scan Pte Ltd
Printed and bound in Italy by Arti Grafiche
Garzanti Verga S.r.l.

10 9 8 7 6 5 4 3 2 1

This book is printed on acid-free paper

CONTENTS

INTRODUCTION 6

TECHNIQUES 9

GLORIOUS GILDING 21

Metal Flower Pots 22

Diamond-patterned Lampshade 24

Gilded Glass Table 28

Two-color Picture Frames 32

Gilded and Découpaged Fruit Bowl 34

Celtic Knot Wall Treatment 39

THE SECRETS OF STENCILING 41

Stenciled Cushion Covers 42

Traditional Wall Treatment 47

Animal Playmat 48

Plaid Jug 53

Stenciled and Stitched Blanket 56

Frosted Mirror 60

PERFECT PAPERCRAFTS 65

Découpaged and Pierced Lampshades 67

Papered and Gilded Chest of Drawers 71

Paper Screen 75

Bathroom Shelf 78

Cutwork Blind 80

PAINTING AND PRINTING 85

Silk Room Divider 87

Printed Velvet Curtains 91

Patterned Bed Linen 94

Checkered Blind 98

MAKING MOSAIC 101

Mosaic Kitchen Pots 103

Basin Splashback 106

Mosaic Mirror 111

Mosaic Garden Table 115

TEMPLATES 118

SUPPLIERS 126

INDEX 127

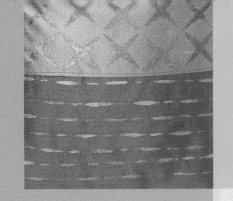

INTRODUCTION

I must confess that I'm addicted to making and decorating.
It doesn't matter what it is; it might be gilding an old lampshade
or making a mosaic pot for the garden. My aim in this book is to
achieve those expensive-looking designer accessories that you can
buy using simple techniques and with no drawn out agony.
Personally, I find that that spoils all the fun. I'm not interested in
complicated projects for people who have endless time on their
hands. I would rather design for those who live in the real world,
where time is at a premium.

I have concentrated on simple techniques that give quick results.
There is the old art of gilding, with it's magical, luxurious finish
that transforms whatever it touches. Or you can try stenciling,
both conventionally on to walls and on to other more unusual
surfaces such as mirrors and china. Simple papercrafts and
painting and printing on to everyday fabrics will turn the plainest
items into works of art. Finally, working with mosaic gives
stunning results with little effort.

Sometimes you need to to take a new look at your home to give
you just a little bit of inspiration. That blind that has been looking
a bit dirty and worn out, why not give it a new lease on life,
see page 98. The battered garden table that you've left outside all
winter, mosaic it and your friends will never believe that it is the
same item, see page 115. Or perhaps your entrance hall is known
as the disaster zone, so paint and gild it in a day, see page 39.
Have fun.

Andrea Maflin

There are no difficult techniques to master

in this book. The following pages explain

the materials you will need and how to use

them (see *Suppliers* on page 126

for any unusual

items). Read these

TECHNIQUES

pages first and always read each project

through before starting – you will

be delighted at how easy and

how much fun it all is.

GLORIOUS GILDING

Metal leaf for gilding comes in two guises, loose and transfer leaf. Loose leaf is quite difficult to master so I use transfer leaf, which comes in books of 25 sheets. Choose from aluminum or copper, both 15 cm (6 in) square, silver, 10 cm (4 in) square, 22ct gold, 8 cm (3 in) square, and Dutch metal (which is gold in color), 15 cm (6 in) square. The leaf is pressed on to pieces of paper, which allows you to cut the leaf to shape, which is impossible with loose leaf. Transfer leaf is more expensive but the extra cost far outweighs the additional time it takes to apply loose leaf.

Size is an oil- or acrylic-based liquid which is brushed over the object to be decorated. It becomes tacky as it dries so the leaf sticks to it. Both types do the same job, although when you clean your brush the oil requires a spirit-based cleaner while the acrylic just needs water. I have used acrylic-based size, which I find easiest to apply with a nylon brush.

The trick is not to put the leaf on to the size too soon; test the size with your fingers to feel if it is tacky. Lay the leaf on top of the size, then gently rub the back of the waxy paper to eliminate any air bubbles. This ensures that all the leaf makes contact with the surface, otherwise some will come off when you rub away the excess. The final drying time depends on the surrounding conditions. On a hot day it may only take an hour, while in damp weather it is best left overnight. To remove excess leaf, simply rub it gently either with your fingers or with a soft, dry cloth.

THE SECRETS OF STENCILING

Stenciling is a wonderful way to create and repeat patterns with ease. You can achieve a professional finish very simply using a wide selection of materials on most surfaces. All the materials can be found in either art shops or DIY stores and if you can hold a craft knife and a brush, you can stencil.

For centuries stencils were cut out of brass or tin plate, but now they are usually made from stencil card. There are two types of stencil card; one yellow in color, the other a buff color. Both are made from manila card which has been soaked in shellac or linseed oil to make it waterproof.

A scalpel or a craft knife with a wooden handle are ideal for cutting the stencil. Make sure you have several spare blades as it is much easier to cut with a sharp knife. A resealing cutting mat is worth investing in as it will protect your surfaces from damage by a knife.

Stencil brushes have short bristles giving a hard, tough surface to stipple with. They do not hold as much paint in the bristles as artist's brushes, and so do not allow too much paint to go through the stencil and create unsightly blobs. Alternatively, you can stencil with a natural sponge or a smooth roller (see pages 47 and 54).

As for the paints, you can use anything from emulsion for walls, to fabric paints that can be bought in art or craft shops, to acrylic artist's paints for the Animal Playmat (see page 48) or frosting varnish for the Frosted Mirror (see page 60).

PERFECT
PAPERCRAFTS

This is one of my favorite mediums as you can completely transform a multitude of surfaces and objects with a layer of paper and glue. Sounds simple? Well, that's because it is. Paper is so undervalued and yet so interesting with all the recycled and handmade varieties available.

I have used three types of paper in this book: layout paper, which is thin and so can be used in layers without becoming too bulky, photocopying paper, and finally watercolor paper which comes in a range of weights, gradually increasing in price the heavier it becomes. All of these are available from art shops.

The glue I have used is PVA, a water-based glue, which usually needs to be diluted before sticking. The exception to this is if you are gluing paper onto glass, then you paint the glue straight onto the glass at full strength. The wonder of PVA is that when it dries it becomes transparent. No specialist paintbrushes are needed, just a normal household brush for large items and a nylon artist's brush for fiddly corners.

PAINTING AND PRINTING

When decorating fabrics, the best results come from using natural materials, like silk or cotton. Experiment on scraps of fabric before starting a whole project. A hot iron on the reverse of the fabric fixes the color but test the heat on the edge first. A piece of paper (not newspaper, as some of the text may come off) can be used to prevent silk and other delicate fabrics from scorching. Wash painted fabrics in a cool wash to maintain the color.

I have worked with concentrated color pigment paints. These have to be mixed with binder before applying to cloth. Be sparing when mixing the pigment with the binder, just one or two drops in half a jam jar of binder will do. I added metallic silver and gold powder to some of the colors for the Silk Room Divider on page 87. Simply mix the metallic powder in, making sure you do not inhale it. See *Suppliers* on page 126 for details of where to buy pigments. If you buy 100 g (4 oz) each of color pigments, 5 kg (11 lb) of pigment binder and 500 grams (20 oz) of metallic powder, you will have enough for all the projects in this book.

Alternatively, ready-mixed fabric paints from art and craft shops work very well on all light-colored materials. I have not used any specialist brushes, a humble household brush is all you need to make lovely brush marks.

MAKING
MOSAIC

Every home has a wall or surface decorated with tiles and we have all probably bought them at some time, but I do find them a bit hard to get excited about, unless they are those really expensive ones. Tiles play an important role in our homes for cool hallway floors, bathroom and shower walls or work tops and walls in the kitchen to provide us with hygienic surfaces, yet they can be very uninspiring.

However, once you have attempted mosaic, you will not be able to stop. I've found it addictive, in a healthy sort of way! I am sorry to keep telling you how easy everything is, but this really is so simple. There is no endless list of materials, all you need are normal bathroom tiles and mosaic tiles, tile clippers, tile cement and the grout. Waterproof grout should be used for projects that will get wet, such as the Basin Splashback on page 106 and the Mosaic Garden Table on page 115.

Mosaic tiles are sold separately in mixed bags or in 30 cm (12 in) square sheets of individual colors. The price varies depending on the color. The front of the tile is coated with paper, which is easily removed by soaking with water. Tile clippers, tile cement and grout can all be bought in a DIY store. You will also find sponges and cloths useful
for wiping away excess grout.

Gilding is the perfect craft; quick and

simple to do, yet giving the most

wonderful results. The plainest lampshade

(see page 24) or most

inexpensive

GLORIOUS GILDING

clip frame (see

page 32) become richly gleaming works

of art, at a fraction of the cost of their

shop-bought counterparts. So be

bold and apply gold.

METAL FLOWER POTS

If you have never tried gilding before, this is the project for you as it is
one you can complete if you have only an hour to spare. My theory is,
if you can pick up a brush then you will be able to gild. No mystery, no tricks,
just instant results. Watch and see how easy it is.

SHOPPING LIST

GALVANIZED METAL POTS

ACRYLIC SIZE

NYLON ARTIST'S PAINTBRUSH

METAL TRANSFER LEAF OF YOUR CHOICE

SOFT RAG

1 Using acrylic size, paint your pattern on
to the tin pot freehand. Try not to be
too concerned with getting the lines perfectly
straight; I prefer a handmade, as opposed to
a manufactured, look. Simply rest your little
finger and the side of your hand on the pot
and run your brush down the length of the pot.
I have used a nylon brush to apply the acrylic
size, but do remember to wash out the brush
with some washing-up liquid; if any size is left
in the brush it will turn as hard as rock.

2 Wait for the size to dry a little so that it
is tacky, this will only take a short time.
Choose which color leaf you want to use;
I have used Dutch metal, silver and copper, all
of which look effective on these pots. Lay a
sheet of transfer leaf over your painted design,
metal side down, and rub the paper backing
gently with your fingertips to push out any air
bubbles that may be underneath the metal leaf.

3 After leaving the pot to dry for an hour
you will be able to rub away any excess
leaf with either your fingers or a soft rag.

DIAMOND-PATTERNED LAMPSHADE

I have always wanted to gild a lampshade ever since
I discovered the shocking price of shop-bought ones.
The gold, or Dutch metal in this case, prevents the light
from penetrating through the card and instead forces it
out though small slits of color left in between each
piece of gold. This shade enhances the atmosphere of a
room by night and reflects the light from its shimmering
surface by day: a most versatile sort of shade.

SHOPPING LIST

LAMPSHADE

CAR SPRAY PAINT

ACRYLIC SIZE

NYLON ARTIST'S PAINTBRUSH

DUTCH METAL TRANSFER LEAF

SCISSORS

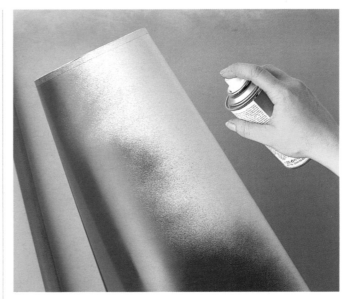

1 Spray the lampshade with car spray paint. I have chosen a strong blue to maximize the contrast with the Dutch metal transfer leaf. Leave to dry.

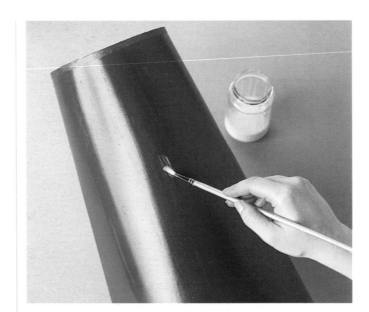

2 Paint on the gold size with a nylon paintbrush. It is worth taking a bit of time to make sure that every part of the shade is covered. Leave to become tacky.

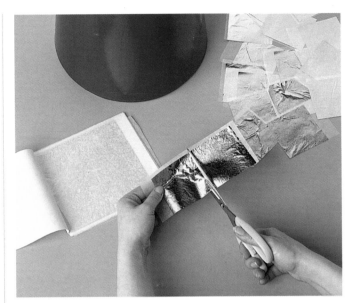

3 Cut each sheet of Dutch metal leaf into quarters. Try to estimate how much you may need and create a small pile to work with.

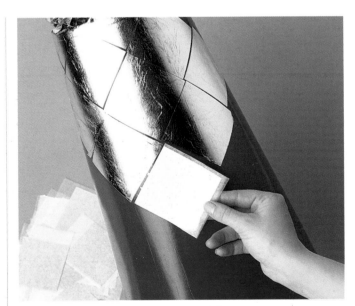

4 Apply the transfer leaf in diamonds working from the top of the shade down towards the bottom, leaving gaps between each piece. Rub each diamond down and remove the backing paper as you go. If you have positioned a piece incorrectly, do not try to remove it. Simply place additional pieces to neaten up the area and continue to finish the shade.

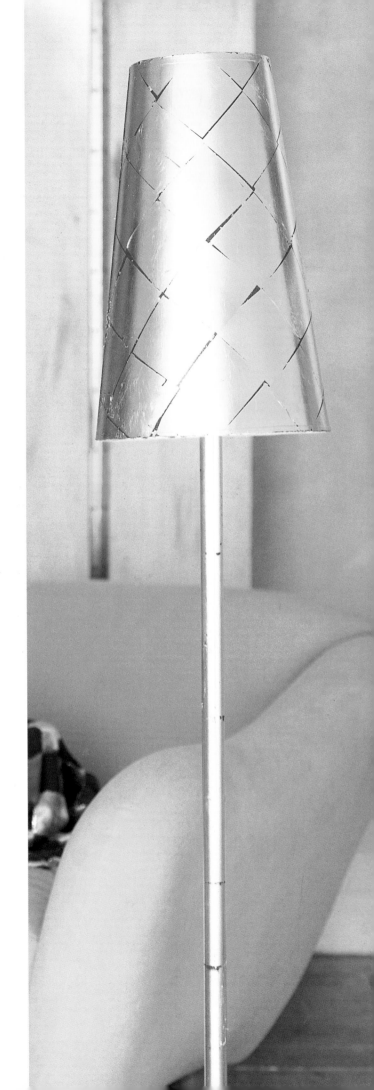

GILDED GLASS TABLE

Sparkling gold and rich azure combine to glorious effect on this easy-to-make
table top. As the decorative finish is underneath the glass it will live happily in the
garden, a perfect excuse for *alfresco* suppers on summer evenings.

SHOPPING LIST

GLASS TABLE TOP

TOWEL

TEMPLATE

STICKY TAPE

NYLON ARTIST'S PAINTBRUSH

ACRYLIC SIZE

DAMP CLOTH

DUTCH METAL TRANSFER LEAF

OLD NEWSPAPERS

CAR SPRAY PAINT

1 Place the glass on a towel to allow you to lift it up easily when the table top is finished. Photocopy the vine template from page 118 a dozen times and position the copies around the edge of the glass. Tape them in place and then turn the glass over. Dip the nylon brush into the acrylic size, not allowing the brush to pick up too much liquid, and trace the vine shapes directly on to the glass (see below). Use the photocopies as a guide only; move the brush freely and interpret the shapes as you go. Only trace two or three shapes at a time. Resting your little finger on the glass will help steady your hand. If you make a mistake simply wipe off the size with a damp cloth. Make sure you have removed all traces of it before you continue. Leave the size for a few minutes to become really tacky before you start to apply the leaf.

TIPS

Take your time when arranging the photocopied templates around the edge of the glass. Measure the circumference of the table and the length of the template (allowing for the space in between each template) and divide one into the other to work out how many templates you will need to photocopy. If necessary, enlarge or reduce the templates until they fit neatly. Alternatively, you could enlarge the template to make one big image and place it in the middle of the glass.

2 Once you have traced over two or three vines with acrylic size, start to apply the Dutch metal transfer leaf. Lay the leaf over the size and, rub it down gently, making sure that all the air bubbles are pushed out to the edges. Continue tracing and laying on the leaf all round the glass.

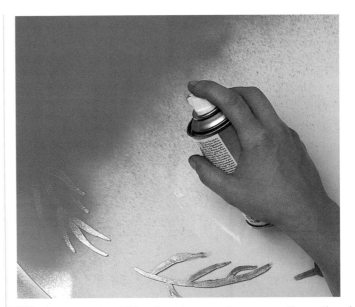

3 Allow the table top to dry overnight. Gently rub your fingers over the transfer leaf to dislodge any excess. Blow the flecks of leaf off the surface.

4 This step should be done in a garden or a well-ventilated area. Cover the work top and surrounding area with old newspaper as you are going to make a mess. Now spray the glass with car paint, covering over the gold leaf. The trick is not to spray too close to the glass as this will create dribbles. Hold the can about 20-25 cm (8-10 in) away from the glass and spray evenly. Allow to dry. Turn the glass over and peel off the photocopies.

VARIATIONS

Bold, fairly simple designs, such as those shown left, work best on the large scale of this table. However, this technique can be used on many glass surfaces; glass shelves or cupboard doors for example. You can also decorate a vase this way, although you do need to place another container inside it to hold the water.

TWO-COLOR PICTURE FRAMES

Clip frames are always useful but could hardly be described as stylish; cheap and cheerful is more honest. You can completely transform and update these humble-looking frames into something quite special and precious with very little effort. Once you have completed one frame you will be ransacking your home to hunt down all those clip frames you put in storage. This technique works on all sizes of frame so why not start small and, as you build confidence, move on to larger-scale projects.

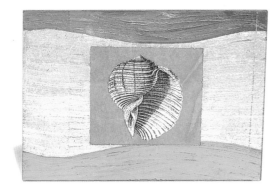

SHOPPING LIST

CLIP FRAME

INVISIBLE STICKY TAPE

CRAFT KNIFE OR SCALPEL

RULER

ACRYLIC SIZE

NYLON ARTIST'S PAINTBRUSH

SILVER TRANSFER LEAF

COPPER TRANSFER LEAF

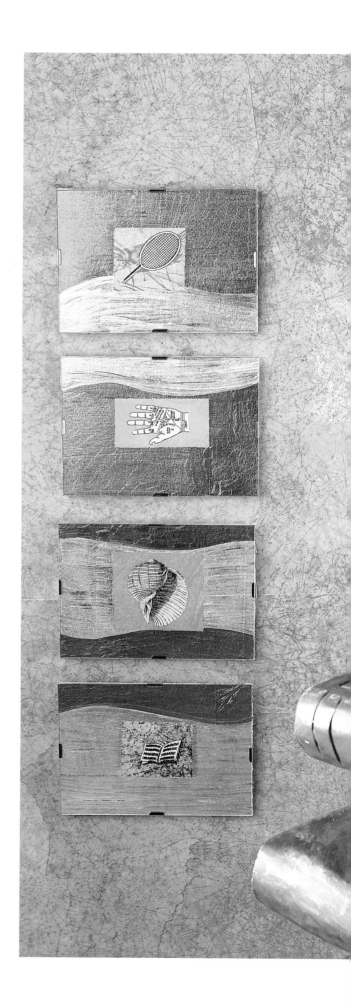

1 Decide on the size of your picture and mask this area off with invisible tape, which will not damage the leaf when you come to remove it. Stick several lengths of tape on to the glass to the required shape, then trim the ends with a craft knife or scalpel and a ruler to give neat edges.

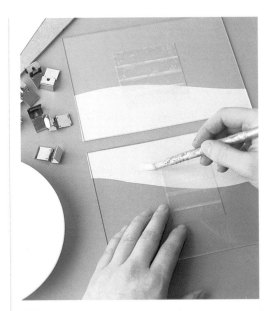

2 Dismantle the frame and cut a piece of white paper to the size of the glass (many frames come with a pre-cut paper backing sheet which is perfect). Draw a curve on the paper and cut it out. Lay it under the frame and, using this as a guide, paint acrylic size on to the glass with a nylon brush. Leave for a few minutes to become tacky.

3 Lay the silver transfer leaf over the size and rub gently to remove air bubbles. Remove the backing and leave to dry. Paint the remainder of the glass with size, overlapping the silver slightly. Leave to dry until tacky. Cover this area with copper transfer leaf and press gently on to the backing to make sure that all areas have made contact with the size.

4 Leave to dry for an hour and then use a craft knife or scalpel to cut away the invisible tape. Work from the middle and carefully peel the tape off from the middle to the edge. Gently rub away any excess leaf from around the edges and across the join.

GILDED AND DÉCOUPAGED FRUIT BOWL

I'm sure we all have a plain glass bowl that someone has given us as a gift, and which has never been let out of the cupboard in which it was first placed. I have used two techniques, gilding and découpage, together to transform something plain into this elegant fruit bowl.

SHOPPING LIST

LAYOUT OR PHOTOCOPYING PAPER

COLD WATER DYE

SMALL LINO ROLLER

CRAFT KNIFE OR SCALPEL

CUTTING MAT

JAM JARS

PVA GLUE

2.5 CM (1 IN) HOUSEHOLD PAINTBRUSH

NYLON ARTIST'S PAINTBRUSH

ACRYLIC SIZE

COPPER TRANSFER LEAF

SILVER TRANSFER LEAF

DRY SOFT CLOTH

1 Choose either layout paper, which is very thin, or photocopying paper which comes a close second. Dilute the cold water dye according to the manufacturer's instructions and roughly wash it over the paper. Then, while the paper is still wet, roll over it with the lino roller to smooth the paint. Leave to dry.

2 Trace the curl shape from the template on page 118 or draw your own shapes. Cut the shapes out of the painted paper with a craft knife or scalpel on a cutting mat.

3 Apply undiluted PVA glue to the inside of the bowl with a household paintbrush. Gently place the shapes colored face down on the glue and smooth out any wrinkles. Leave to dry until the glue becomes transparent.

4 Use a nylon brush to paint the inside of the bowl with acrylic size. Leave for a few minutes to become tacky. Then stick copper transfer leaf over the whole of the inside of the bowl, covering the paper shapes and smoothing out any air bubbles. Don't be too concerned if cracks appear in the leaf, simply put more leaf on.

5 Paint patterns on to the outside of the bowl with a nylon brush dipped in acrylic size, concentrating on the paper parts of the design. Apply the silver leaf over the patterns. Leave the size to dry then rub away the excess from both the inside and outside of the bowl with either your fingers or a dry soft cloth.

TIPS

I once tried to scrub off the finish on a bowl like this with water, and it took quite a lot of effort. However, you can make your bowl even more hardwearing by painting the inside with an oil-based varnish. Leave it to dry in a well-ventilated area for several days and make sure that the smell has completely disappeared before you fill the bowl with fruit.

CELTIC KNOT
WALL TREATMENT

Gilding on to walls creates a really luxurious look for very little money and effort. Light, natural or artificial, reflects off the metallic motifs, adding a warm glow to the whole room. You'll never go back to plain old wallpaper again. For the most dramatic effect, first paint the wall in a strong shade to contrast with your transfer leaf.

SHOPPING LIST

TEMPLATES

STENCIL CARD

PEN

CRAFT KNIFE OR SCALPEL

CUTTING MAT

LOW-TACK TAPE

NYLON ARTIST'S PAINTBRUSH

ACRYLIC SIZE

COPPER TRANSFER LEAF

DRY SOFT CLOTH

1 Trace off the three templates on page 119. Transfer the designs to stencil card (see page 118) and cut them out. Position the stencils on the wall, using low-tack tape to keep them in place. With a nylon artist's paintbrush, paint the stencils one at a time with acrylic size.

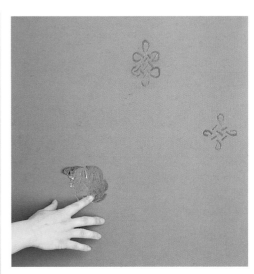

2 Remove the stencil, allow the size to become tacky, then place the copper transfer leaf over the size. Rub gently, making contact with the size. Peel away the backing of the transfer leaf. Leave to dry; it may take a few hours for the size to harden.

3 Rub away the excess leaf with fingers or a soft cloth. Repeat with the other designs.

Stenciling is a popular craft that is both

simple to do and gives quick results: perfect!

I have used it to give a new lease on life to

cushion covers and a blanket

and, slightly

THE SECRETS OF STENCILING

more unusually,

to plain china and a mirror. I also show how

to make a child's playmat decorated with

colorful animals.

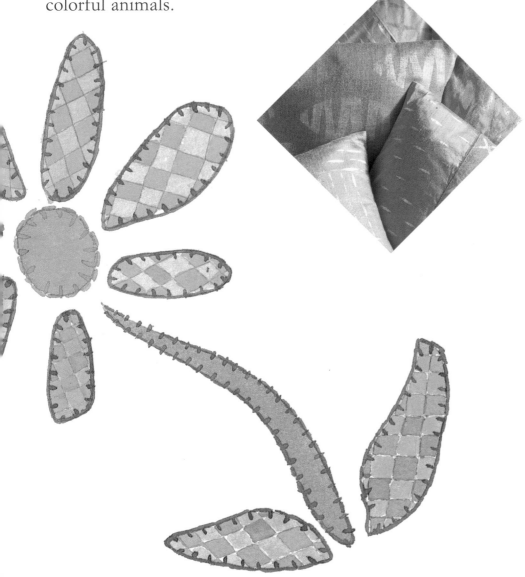

STENCILED
CUSHION COVERS

Fabric paints can be fixed with a hot iron after which they
are machine washable, so this is both a beautiful and
practical way to decorate a cushion cover. You can
embellish a ready-made cover, and there are many shapes and
sizes available in all kinds of fabrics from department
stores and home-furnishing shops. Place a piece of card
inside the cover before you begin to stop the paint
going through to the back of the cover.

Alternatively you can make up your own cushion.
This is very simple as all you need are two pieces of fabric
the size of your cushion pad
and a zip. You can make
the front of the cushion
from two or more different
colored pieces of fabric
pieced together.

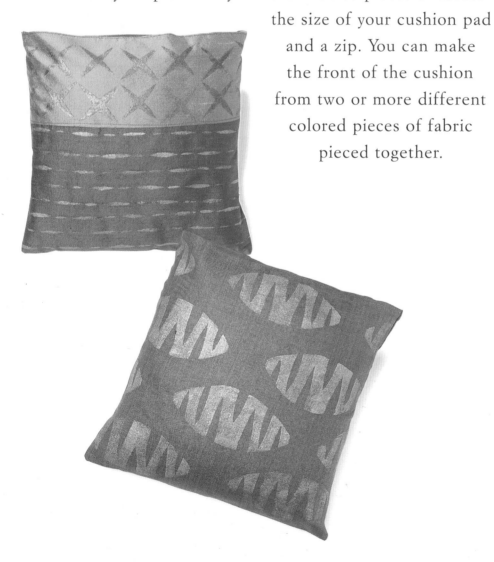

SHOPPING LIST

- **CUSHION PAD**
- **TAPE MEASURE**
- **FABRIC**
- **STENCIL CARD**
- **PENCIL**
- **CRAFT KNIFE OR SCALPEL**
- **CUTTING MAT**
- **FABRIC PAINTS IN SILVERY-BLUE AND GOLD**
- **SAUCERS**
- **STENCIL BRUSHES**
- **IRON**
- **NEEDLE AND THREAD OR SEWING MACHINE**
- **ZIP OR POPPER TAPE**

1 Measure your cushion pad and cut the fabric to size allowing a 5 cm (2 in) seam allowance. This is a little wider than usual but you may need the extra space to position your design to best advantage on the cushion. Either copy a design from pages 119 and 120 and transfer it on to the stencil card (see page 118), or draw up your own design; a saucer is a useful alternative to a compass when it comes to drawing curves. Cut out the stencil with a sharp craft knife or scalpel on a cutting mat.

2 Put a small quantity of silvery-blue fabric paint on a saucer and dab the stencil brush into it. It is important not to get too much paint on the brush or it will seep under the card and create blobs. If you have not stenciled before then try it out on a piece of scrap fabric first. Lay the card on the fabric and hold firmly in place. With stabbing motions dab the paint through the cut outs in the stencil card. Lift the card off the fabric when you have finished and allow the fabric and card to dry.

3 Lay the stencil card over your design again but do not line it up exactly. Stencil again in gold. Leave it to dry.

4 With a hot dry iron, iron the back of the fabric to fix the paint. Make up the cushion inserting a zip or popper tape along one edge. Once you are confident with the technique, why not try designing some curtains or table linen.

TRADITIONAL
WALL TREATMENT

In this room I have some large pieces of furniture so I did not want anything too fiddly on the walls. Taking my inspiration from a 16th-century fabric design, I simply enlarged my chosen pattern to the desired size. You could decorate a whole room in a day quite easily using this technique.

SHOPPING LIST

STENCIL CARD

PENCIL

CRAFT KNIFE OR SCALPEL

CUTTING BOARD

LOW-TACK TAPE

EMULSION PAINT IN TWO SHADES OF THE SAME COLOR

PLATE

NATURAL SPONGE

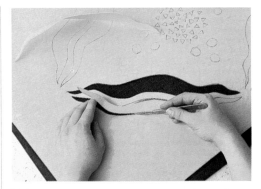

1 Spend some time choosing the right pattern for your walls and deciding on the arrangement of the stenciled motifs. Use the template on page 121 or create your own design. You do not have to be a genius to make a stencil. Sketch or photocopy a design from a book or magazine; when you start to look you will see patterns everywhere. Enlarge it on a photocopier to the desired size and trace it on to stencil card (see page 118). Cut out the stencil carefully with a craft knife or scalpel on a cutting board.

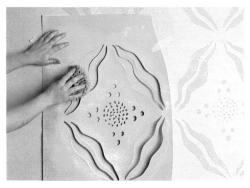

2 Tape the stencil to the wall. Pour some paint on to a plate then, using a natural sponge, gently dab the color though the stencil, producing a soft texture rather than a solid color. Leave to dry.

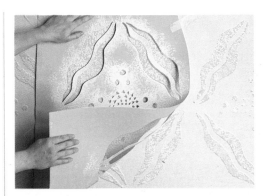

3 Repeat the process with a lighter color, this time dabbing the paint on more randomly, allowing some of the first color to come though. Remember not to smudge the last stencil as you continue along the wall.

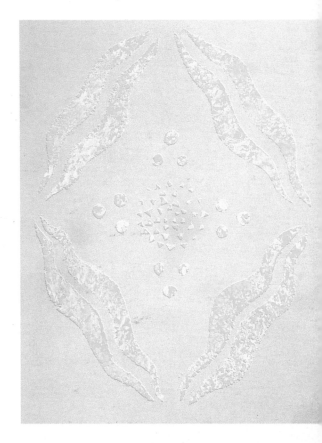

ANIMAL PLAYMAT

I must admit I had a lot of fun making this child's playmat. If the truth be known I would be quite happy placing it next to some of my more grown-up possessions.

This project is all about color; choose three or four fresh, bright colors and mix them with each other and with white to create further shades. This way you will find that the colors will sit happily together. Spend a little time considering the stencil shapes and deciding upon the arrangement you like before you start stenciling.

SHOPPING LIST

CANVAS MATERIAL

LARGE PAINTBRUSH

GESSO OR WHITE PRIMER PAINT

RULER

PENCIL

LOW-TACK TAPE

ACRYLIC PAINTS

STENCIL CARD

CRAFT KNIFE OR SCALPEL

CUTTING MAT

SAUCERS

STENCIL BRUSHES

1 Cut out a rectangle of canvas 150 cm (59 in) by 120 cm (48 in). Use a large paintbrush to paint the whole surface with a coat of gesso or white primer and leave to dry.

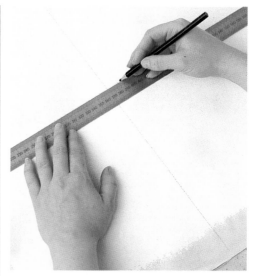

2 With a ruler and a pencil draw a border 30 cm (12 in) from each edge, extending each line to the edge of the canvas thus creating a rectangle in the middle of the canvas and a square at each corner.

3 Experiment with the colors you want to use and have them ready mixed before you start. Mask off each area in turn with low-tack tape and paint the colors on with a large paintbrush. Leave to dry.

5 Cut large irregular shapes from stencil card to fit within the central panel. Place some of the negative stencils inside some of these shapes and stencil them on to the canvas. Pour some paint into a saucer and just dip the brush into it, without getting too much paint on to the brush – test it before you start on the painted canvas.

4 Photocopy the templates on pages 122-124 and transfer them on to stencil card (see page 118). Cut out the stencils carefully with a craft knife or scalpel on a cutting mat.

I have made three different types of animal stencil:

1 The positive shape of the animal, which is the one I'm about to cut out in the photograph above.
2 The negative shape of the same animal.
3 The detail of the animal with its markings and outline.

6 With your positive stencils paint the background colors of the animals around the border. When dry, it's time to add the detail. Position the stencil and gently apply the paint with a soft stabbing motion. I mixed different colors for the detail stencil, a candy floss pink and a grass green.

PLAID JUG

Plain china is easily accessible and timeless, but it
can be fun to give a face lift to items you have
had around for a while.

I have always admired tartan-style and checkered pottery,
with its layering of color and simple application of pattern.
Simplicity is often the hardest thing to achieve and personally
I find it the most satisfying. These ceramic paints
won't stand too much washing and shouldn't be used on
surfaces that come into contact with food, so use
them to paint vases, the outsides of fruit bowls, or as here,
a decorative jug.

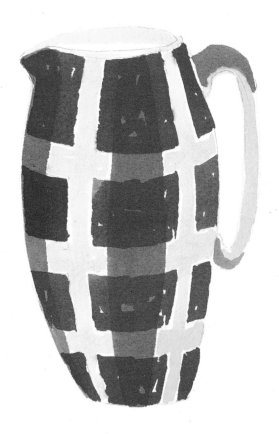

SHOPPING LIST

PLAIN CHINA JUG

5 CM (2 IN) WIDE LOW-TACK TAPE

2.5 CM (1 IN) WIDE LOW-TACK TAPE

CERAMIC PAINTS IN TWO SHADES OF THE SAME COLOR

ACRYLIC PAINTBRUSH

SPONGE ROLLER

COTTON SWAB

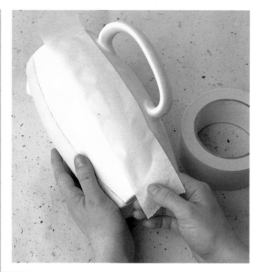

1 I have used two widths of masking tapes to achieve this checkered effect. Start with 5 cm (2 in) tape and stick on four strips running down the jug at equal intervals. Take a bit of time to make sure that the edge of the tape has made contact with the jug.

2 Paint ceramic paint in between the tape strips with a paintbrush. I have used an acrylic brush because it is soft and holds a lot of paint in its bristles.

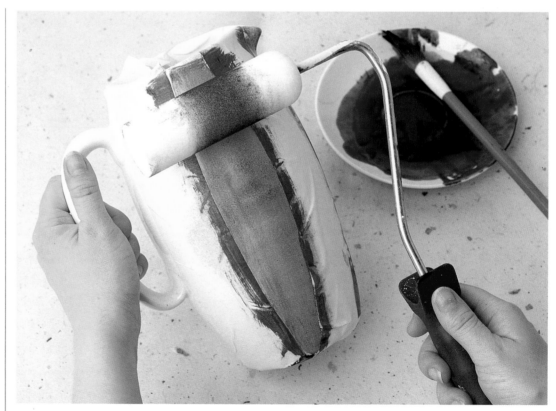

3 While the paint is still wet, roll over each area with a clean sponge roller to distribute the paint evenly. When dry, remove the tape.

4 Repeat the whole process but this time, use the 2.5 cm (1 in) tape. Stick the tape in the center of the white areas going down the jug and in three stripes going around the jug. Apply a darker version of the same color with the brush and then roller it. When dry, remove the tape. If the paint has seeped under the edge of the masking tape, simply clean the area with a cotton swab. Paint a stripe down the handle to complete the transformation.

STENCILED AND STITCHED BLANKET

Conjure up a sumptuous blanket that can be used indoors as a throw for a sofa or comfortable chair or as a picnic rug on a gloriously hot day in the country.

This would be a good project to start with if you have never tried stenciling before as the felt is both easy to work on and to cut out while the appliqué is done with simple blanket stitch.

SHOPPING LIST

STENCIL CARD

CRAFT KNIFE OR
SCALPEL

RULER

PENCIL

20 CM (8 IN)
SQUARES OF COLORED
FELT

FABRIC PAINT

SAUCER

STENCIL BRUSH

IRON

SCISSORS

WOOLEN BLANKET

PINS

WOOLEN EMBROIDERY
THREAD

EMBROIDERY NEEDLE

1 Cut a piece of stencil card about 20 cm (8 in) square and draw a 1 cm (½ in) grid on to it. Cut out alternate squares to make a gingham pattern, leaving a solid border of 2.5 cm (1 in) to give the stencil strength.

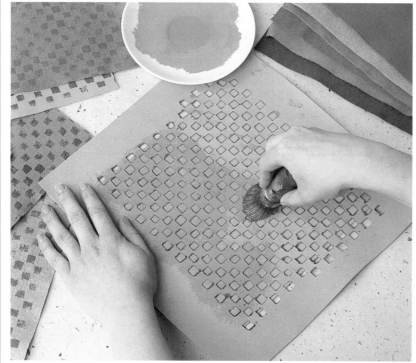

2 Place the felt on a work surface which can be wiped down later. Pour a little fabric paint onto a saucer and dip the tip of the stencil brush in to it, being careful not to flood the brush with fabric paint, otherwise the paint may go under the stencil card and create unsightly blobs. Lay the stencil on the felt and with firm dabbing movements stencil the paint through the card. Leave to dry. Iron the back of the felt with a hot iron to fix the paint.

58

VARIATIONS

Use some of the animals from the playmat on page 48 to make a blanket for your children's room. Stencil the shapes on to felt and sew them on with brightly colored wool.

3 Trace off the templates on page 125 and cut out the felt shapes. You will need five petals, one stem and one or two leaves for each flower. Arrange the flowers on the woolen blanket and when you are happy with the design pin them in place.

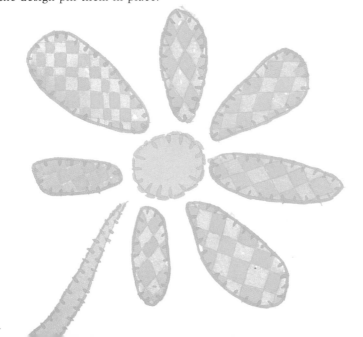

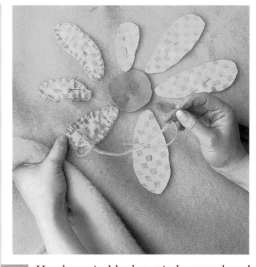

4 Hand sew in blanket stitch around each element of each flower with woolen embroidery thread in a contrasting color.

FROSTED MIRROR

This mirror has been a real success story for me.
Friends ask me where I bought it from and when I tell them
that I made it they pause for thought, then ask me how!
Even those friends of mine who would never normally
get their hands dirty have been inspired to try this project
as it really is so simple and so stunning. They disappear
clutching their instructions, all ready to get started.

SHOPPING LIST

MIRROR WITH GROUND EDGES, CUT TO SIZE

5 CM (2 IN) WIDE LOW-TACK TAPE

RULER

MARKER PEN

CRAFT KNIFE OR SCALPEL

PLATE

TURQUOISE GLASS PAINT

FROSTING VARNISH

SPONGE ROLLER

1 Cover the whole mirror with low-tack tape, I have used 5 cm (2 in) tape but any width will do.

2 Measure the width you would like your stenciled border and with a marker pen draw in the central circle. Draw the wavy lines; I have done this freehand, although you could measure them out. Draw right across the mirror as the lines will flow better that way, then crosshatch between the lines within the border to remind you to stencil the hatched areas only.

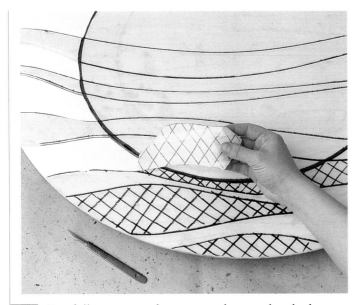

3 Carefully cut away the tape on the crosshatched areas with a craft knife or scalpel. It is important not to remove the tape on the center circle.

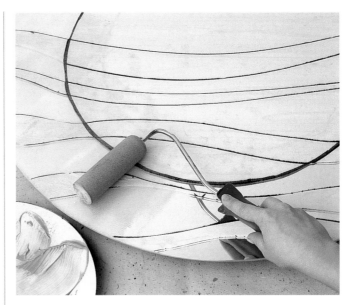

4 On a plate mix a small amount of turquoise glass paint with the frosting varnish; experiment until you get a pale, ice-blue color. With a sponge roller apply the mixture of frosting varnish and glass paint evenly to all the areas of bare mirror. The sponge eats up a lot of the mixture so make up a reasonable amount to cover all the mirror.

VARIATIONS

You can use this technique to frost anything made from glass, though don't use it on drinking glasses or glass plates as the paint should not come into contact with food. As an alternative to net curtains, try frosting a bathroom or kitchen window. Mask off designs with tape as shown here, or cut a mask from sticky-backed plastic. Simple geometric shapes work well, though as you get more confident you might try frosting your monogram onto a window.

5 I found the best time to remove the tape is before the varnish mixture has dried completely. Peel away the tape carefully and leave to dry. If you need to, you can touch up the paint with a fine brush.

Paper is such a wonderful decorating medium as it is inexpensive, readily available and easy to work with. Paper will also cover a multitude of sins so a battered chest of drawers (see page 71) can be given a facelift with none of the painstaking preparation work necessary if you repaint.

PERFECT PAPERCRAFTS

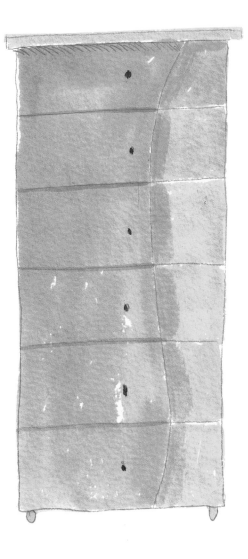

DÉCOUPAGED AND PIERCED LAMPSHADES

Lighting makes a real difference to the character of a room,
and adds an interesting element to your home.
Recycle an old shade or buy a cheap one and transform it
with one of these simple techniques.

Photocopy the flowers on these pages or use patterns from
magazines or books to make the découpaged shade.
You can pierce any fairly simple shape on to a lampshade;
stars, geometric designs or even your initials will work well.

SHOPPING LIST

LAMPSHADE

SHEET OF HANDMADE PAPER BIG ENOUGH TO COVER THE SHADE

PENCIL

SCISSORS

PVA GLUE

2.5 CM (1 IN) HOUSEHOLD PAINTBRUSH

PHOTOCOPIED IMAGES

TEA BAG

FIRE RETARDANT SPRAY

BRADLE OR SKEWER

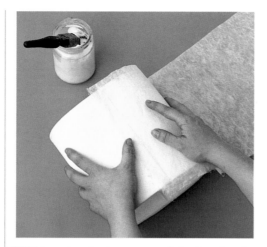

1 Lay the shade on top of the handmade paper and roll it round from seam to seam. With a pencil carefully draw around the top and bottom of the shade. Cut out the paper pattern. Dilute PVA to the consistency of single cream and cover the outside of the lampshade with an even coat. Gently stick the paper to the shade. You may need to brush it very gently with a damp brush to eliminate any air bubbles. Leave it to dry.

2 Photocopy your chosen images. I have used floral etchings which have a lot of detail. Enlarge or reduce them to fit the scale of your shade. You can create an interesting effect by changing the scale of the images in relation to each other as well. Put a tea bag into quarter of a cup of boiling water and leave it to stew. Paint some of the photocopies with the tea and leave some white.

3 Apply the glue to the face of the photocopies and stick them inside the shade. Spray the inside of the shade with fire retardant. Once lit, the shade will be transformed as the images will shine through.

4 To make a pierced shade, follow step one. Pierce the shade with a bradle or skewer at regular intervals. You can measure out where you want each hole to go, although I did this shade by eye.

VARIATIONS

Cut small crosses approximately 1 cm (½ in) square into the lampshade with a craft knife or scalpel. From the inside push your finger through the cross, forcing the cut pieces to part. When the lamp is turned on, the light will shine through as bold as brass.

PAPERED AND GILDED CHEST OF DRAWERS

The word storage can conjure up anything from a mixture of stark minimalist settings at one extreme, to rampant clutter at the other. I should think that most of us are looking for the middle ground, a system to help us fight the battle to keep our lives in reasonable order. It seems a shame not to give a little bit of attention to making storage more attractive.

Ideal for those with hoarder's instinct, this chest of drawers is a decorative piece that deserves all the attention it will get.

SHOPPING LIST

COLD WATER DYES

LAYOUT PAPER, ENOUGH TO COVER THE WHOLE CHEST

ACRYLIC PAINTBRUSH

SAUCERS

SALT

SCISSORS

SANDPAPER

PVA GLUE

2.5 CM (1 IN) HOUSEHOLD PAINTBRUSH

PENCIL

ACRYLIC SIZE

NYLON ARTIST'S PAINTBRUSH

DUTCH METAL TRANSFER LEAF

SOFT DRY CLOTH

1 I used cold water fabric dyes as the salt technique will not work with any other medium and the colors are so intense. I chose a color theme of blue; the color graduates from light greeny-blue at the top to a royal blue at the bottom. Paint some spare paper to make sure the colors you have chosen work together; the trick is not to make the colors too different from one another. You must wait until the paper is dry to get the full effect. You will need one sheet of paper for each drawer and sheets to cover the top and sides of the chest. Mix the dyes and pour some of each color into a saucer. Paint half of each sheet with one color and, while wet, paint the other half with another color, allowing the two colors to bleed into each other.

2 Lay the papers where they can dry undisturbed. Sprinkle them with salt and leave to dry. When they are completely dry, brush off any remaining salt residue.

3 Lay each sheet over a drawer front and crease the paper around the edges of the drawer to create a template. Do the same for the top and sides of the chest of drawers. Cut out the paper shapes with a pair of scissors.

4 Sand the chest to make sure there is no varnish or polish left on the surface of the wood. Coat a drawer front with a thin layer of PVA diluted to half thickness with water. Coat the reverse of the paper with glue and apply the paper to the drawer. Repeat on each drawer and the sides and top of the chest of drawers. Leave to dry.

5 Once the drawers have been covered with the decorated papers, put the drawers into the chest and draw a wavy line in pencil down the front a quarter of the distance across the front. Paint the smaller area with size and leave it to become tacky.

6 Apply the Dutch metal transfer leaf. As you apply the leaf rub it gently with your fingers to create cracks in the leaf allowing the paper finish to show beneath. Leave to dry for a few hours, then rub away any excess metal leaf with a dry soft cloth.

PAPER SCREEN

This is the most fiddly project in this book, so I do warn you that it cannot be undertaken in a rush, it has to be looked on as a labor of love. Now that I have completely put you off doing this project I would like, in the same breath, to say that anyone who visits you will immediately be drawn to this delicious fruit-colored screen. It masks off an area for privacy perfectly or screens a not-so-lovely view without sacrificing any light.

I used the frame of an old fabric-covered screen for this project. I stripped off the worn covering and painted the wood with emulsion paint. If you cannot find a suitable frame you could make one very simply from strips of timber screwed together to make a rectangle; make three of these and hinge them together. Measure the size of your screen and work out how many cards you will need to fill it; 10 A1-size sheets of watercolor paper provided enough for this frame.

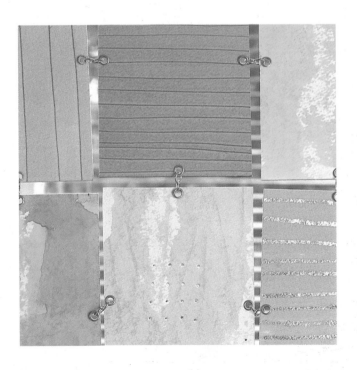

SHOPPING LIST

10 A1 SHEETS OF HEAVY WATERCOLOR PAPER

COLD WATER DYES

SAUCER

SMALL LINO ROLLER

5 CM (2 IN) HOUSEHOLD PAINTBRUSH

RULER

CRAFT KNIFE OR SCALPEL

CUTTING MAT

ACRYLIC SIZE

SILVER TRANSFER LEAF

BRADAWL OR SKEWER

5 MM (¼ IN) COMBINATION PLIERS

EYELETS

9 MM (½ IN) BROKEN RINGS

JEWELERY PLIERS

1 There are two methods of coloring the paper. Pour a small quantity of cold water dye into a saucer, cover the lino roller with the dye and roll on to the paper. Repeat the process until the paper is covered with broken color.

2 Alternatively, dip the household paintbrush into the dye, being careful not to fill the brush with too much liquid. Gently drag it across the paper. Repeat until you have covered the paper.

VARIATIONS

This technique can also be used to make a fixed blind or a wallhanging.

For a blind, measure your window frame and work out the number of cards you will need. Make up the blind as for the screen. Screw eyelets into the top of the window frame and hang the blind from them.

For a wallhanging, screw the eyelets into a wooden batten painted to match the wall and mount this on the wall with screws.

3 Work out how many 10 cm (4 in) x 15 cm (6 in) cards you will need and cut the colored papers into the required number. You can now embellish the cards with gilding, scoring and piercing.

4 Gilding – paint your pattern on to the card with acrylic size, apply the silver leaf and rub away the excess.

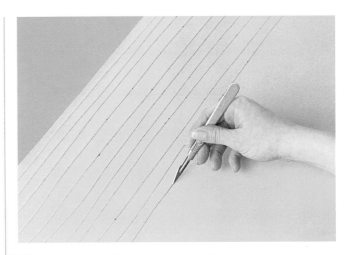

5 Scoring – while the paper is still wet score it with a craft knife or scalpel.

6 Piercing – hold the paper firmly while you pierce patterns in it with a bradawl or skewer.

7 On each card make a hole in the center of each side with your combination pliers. Place an eyelet in each hole and squeeze the pliers together across the eyelet to fix it in place. Repeat the process in each hole of each piece of card. This does take time but it is not difficult to do.

8 Lay out your papers in a grid pattern and when you are happy with the arrangement, begin to join the cards together. Use 9 mm (½ in) metal broken rings that can be squeezed shut with small pliers to build a chainmail screen. Repeat until you have joined enough cards to fill each panel of the screen. To join the papers to the wooden frame, screw eyelets into the frame opposite the top and bottom of each card and opposite alternate cards on the sides.

BATHROOM SHELF

Glass sounds a rather scary sort of material to decorate. However, this technique is really simple and can in fact be used to cover a multitude of surfaces, so you could start to co-ordinate the look in other areas in the same room, using different colors to cover a panelled door or a cupboard or a lampshade. Apply the paper in the same way with the same glue, the only limitation is your imagination.

SHOPPING LIST

WAX CANDLE

BOARD OR THICK CARD

LAYOUT PAPER

COLD WATER DYE

FINE SANDPAPER

PVA GLUE

2.5 CM (1 IN) HOUSEHOLD PAINTBRUSH

GLASS SHELF CUT TO SIZE WITH GROUND EDGES

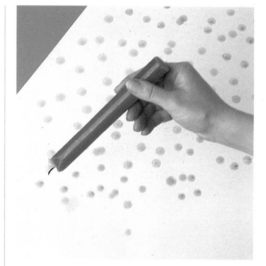

1 Drip melted candle wax over a piece of board or thick card. This will make the pattern that you will transfer onto the paper.

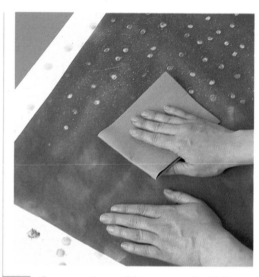

2 Cover a piece of layout paper with a wash of cold water dye. Once dry, lay the paper face up on top of the melted wax pattern. With some fine sandpaper gently sand away the color to reveal the textured pattern.

3 With neat PVA glue stick the paper to the glass face down. Paper bubbles when wet, so you need to smooth it out. Leave it to dry.

CUTWORK BLIND

We rarely notice everyday items such as roller blinds in our hectic lives. Simple by design, functional, neatly folding away when not required, blinds are very practical but not much fun. With an hour or two to spare you can change all this.

Light has a terrific impact on our wellbeing and this project will update a window and bring a startling change to the whole room, transforming it with beams of light, yet this blind is easily achievable and requires no special tools.

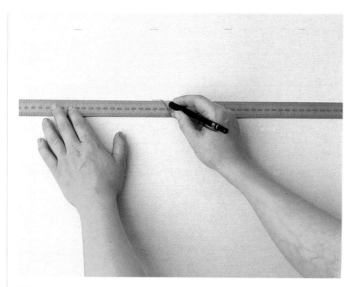

1 Lay out your blind face down. Measure the blind across and down. Allow 10 cm (4 in) on each side and at the top and bottom for the border. Work from the top down.

With a pencil, mark a 1cm (½ in) line every 10 cm (4 in). The final result is a grid of small dashes in lines going across and down the blind. These dashes create the bases of the squares to be cut out.

2 Place a cutting mat underneath the blind. Starting on the pencil line follow the line with your scapel. Continue by cutting two 1 cm (½ in) lines vertically on either side of the pencil line to make the sides of the square. The cut across the top finishes the square. Cut all the squares out.

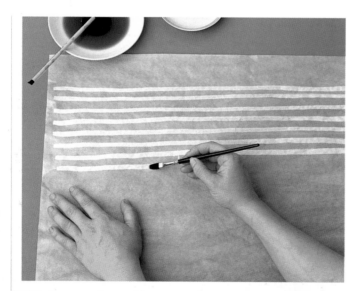

3 Cover a sheet of layout paper with a wash of cold water fabric dye and leave it to dry. Pour some household bleach into a saucer and with a flat artist's paintbrush, paint stripes across the paper with the bleach. The dye color will instantly disappear. Paint more stripes down the paper to create a checkered pattern.

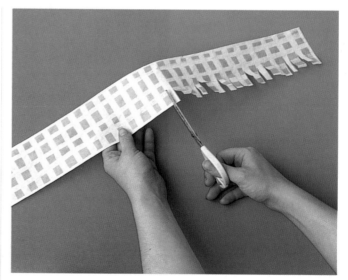

4 Cut a strip of the paper wide enough to fit across the bottom of your blind by 10 cm (4 in) deep. With scissors cut a the bottom third of this strip into a fringe. Stick the paper to the lower edge of the blind with double-sided tape. Leave to dry then hang the blind.

VARIATIONS

Simple geometric shapes are best for this technique; triangles or diamonds work well. If you are unsure, draw the pattern out on paper and hang it on the wall to see how it looks from a distance.

SHOPPING LIST

ROLLER BLIND

PENCIL AND RULER

CUTTING MAT

CRAFT KNIFE
OR SCALPEL

LAYOUT PAPER

COLD WATER DYE

HOUSEHOLD BLEACH

SAUCER

FLAT ARTIST'S BRUSH

SCISSORS

DOUBLE-SIDED TAPE

These are probably the simplest techniques in the book and by painting on to acetate and then printing on to fabric you greatly reduce the chances of making a mistake. All the projects

in this section are quite large, but don't be nervous. Experiment on scraps of fabric until you are ready to move on.

SILK ROOM DIVIDER

You can so easily enhance your living space by using hand-printed fabrics to divide up a room. Screen off that ever-growing pile of children's toys or divide off a kitchen in an open plan area.

Silk gives a rich luxurious look and is easy to print on. However, plain cotton will also work well and has a more utilitarian feel. I have used fabric pigments which are best for strongly colored fabrics, though ordinary fabric paints will work equally well on light-colored materials. Experiment on scraps first to see how the colors look before you start the project.

SHOPPING LIST

STRIPS OF FABRIC OF VARYING LENGTHS AND THE WIDTH OF YOUR DIVIDER

SEWING MACHINE

TEA TOWEL

IRON

LOW-TACK TAPE

AN A2-SIZED PIECE OF ACETATE

HOUSEHOLD PAINTBRUSH

PIGMENTS IN YELLOW, PINK, ULTRAMARINE, BLUE, BLACK, WHITE AND TURQUOISE AND PIGMENT BINDER OR FABRIC PAINTS IN THESE COLORS

METALLIC POWDER OR METALLIC FABRIC PAINT

METAL CANS OR JAM JARS TO MIX PIGMENTS IN

SAUCER

PENCIL

LAYOUT PAPER OR SUGAR PAPER

CRAFT KNIFE, SCALPEL OR SCISSORS

EYELET KIT

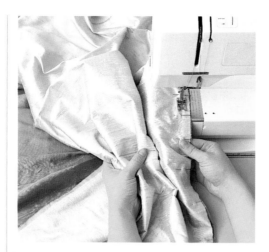

1 Stitch the fabric strips together to make one piece the size you would like your divider to be. Turn under and stitch down the raw edges on the back as both sides of the fabric will be on show. Press the seams through a damp tea towel.

Your work surface must be clean and free from grease. It will need to be as wide as your fabric but not as long. Concentrate on printing one part of the fabric length at a time. Lay your fabric over your work surface and attach low-tack tape at intervals down each side of the fabric to prevent it from moving.

2 Paint patterns directly on to the acetate with a household brush. Be reasonably liberal with the paint and allow the brush stokes to show as they will add texture to the pattern. Experiment on a spare piece of cloth to gauge how much fabric paint needs to be applied. Also experiment by painting only patches of the acetate rather than covering it all.

3 Drag the handle end of the brush across the painted acetate adding lines to the overall effect. If you make a mistake, simply wipe the acetate clean and start again. It is important to apply the painted acetate to the fabric without delay as the paint will start to dry.

4 Place the acetate face down on to the fabric. Smooth it out to eliminate any air pockets. Peel the acetate gently away to reveal the pattern. Wash the acetate and let it dry before printing the next section of the divider. The template for the coiled design is on page 125.

5 Trace round a saucer on paper several times and then cut out the circles with a scalpel or scissors. Lay the circles on the cloth. Coat the acetate with fabric paint, then smooth this onto the fabric. Gently peel back the acetate, the paper circles will stick to it and peel away. Wash the acetate with a damp cloth. Leave to dry. If you drop a little paint onto the cloth by mistake, leave it to dry. Do not be tempted to wipe it with a damp cloth as this only makes matters worse.

6 To hang the divider from a pole or wire, punch metal eyelets into the top hem. You can buy an eyelet kit from a haberdashery shop and it is simple to use if you follow the manufacturer's instructions.

TIPS

Choose any pattern or texture that appears on other items in your room and use it on the dividers to give a fully co-ordinated look and style.

PRINTED VELVET CURTAINS

Sumptuous curtains such as these look ambitious,
but I'm not interested in designing long, agonizing, drawn-out
projects that take over your life for a week or so.
Very few of us can afford that luxury. So, what looks at first
glance as if it requires experience and understanding
of painting on fabric, could not be further from the truth.

Curtain-making in itself seems a scary subject if you're
not a seamstress, but all I have done is print on to a pair of
old, plain curtains and add a contrasting-colored hem and
trimming. This is also an excellent way of recycling a pair of
curtains as you simply make the hem as wide as is needed
to make the curtains fit the window. Don't be put off by the
scale of this project – it is the easiest in this chapter.
However, I will leave it to your discretion as to whether you
tell your admirers the same story.

SHOPPING LIST

OLD, PLAIN CURTAINS

CONTRASTING FABRIC

TASSEL TRIM

SEWING MACHINE

SEWING THREADS

ACETATE

A4 PAPER

PIGMENTS AND
PIGMENT BINDER OR
FABRIC PAINTS

SAUCERS TO HOLD
FABRIC PAINT

5 CM (2 IN)
PAINTBRUSH

4 CM (1½ IN)
PAINTBRUSH

NYLON ARTIST'S
PAINTBRUSH

IRON

1 Before you start printing, make up the curtains. Measure the depth of the window and sew a deep border in a contrasting colored fabric (I have used green velvet) to the bottom of the curtains to make them the right length. Sew on the tassel trim to cover the join.

Cut pieces of paper 20 cm (8 in) square. Arrange them in a simple pattern on top of the main curtains in the places you want to print.

2 Cut out a piece of acetate 30cm (12 in) square. Position the acetate over a paper square and paint directly on to the acetate with a 5 cm (2 in) household paintbrush, over the paper square. Remove the paper square and place the painted acetate face down on the fabric where the paper was positioned. Rub the back of the acetate so that it make contact with the fabric. Peel away, paint and re-position until all of the paper squares have been replaced with printed squares.

3 Repeat the same process but with a soft gold paint. This time make a smaller square. Place the acetate on to the fabric, paint the square with the smaller paintbrush in the same fashion as before. Turn the acetate over and rub the reverse. Repeat until all of the colored squares are complete.

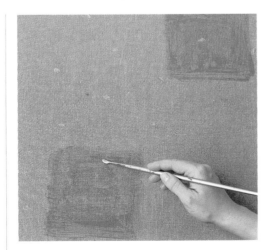

4 With a nylon artist's paintbrush, paint random gold dots all over the fabric. These will take longer to dry than the squares.

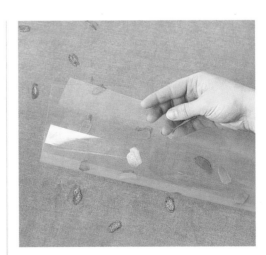

5 Now decorate the hem. With the nylon artist's paintbrush, paint larger dashes over the acetate. Place the acetate face down on to the velvet. Rub the back of the acetate firmly to make contact with the fabric. Repeat until the pattern is complete. Iron the back of the curtains to fix the paint and they are ready to be hung up.

PATTERNED BED LINEN

Fashion designers have finally found the allure of our homes more than they can resist, and have started to design our interiors as well as our clothes. Bed linen has become a real favorite, unfortunately at a cost. However, you can transform a plain duvet cover with ease by printing it.

Don't be fearful of the scale of the project, just flip through the steps to see how easy it is to achieve. I made the duvet by stitching two bed sheets together, having printed one of them first. If you want to decorate a ready-made cover you must slip a layer of folded paper inside it to prevent the paint marking the back of the cover.

SHOPPING LIST

Two bed sheets, big enough to cover your duvet

A2 paper, you could use newspaper or recycled paper

Marker pen

Three sheets of acetate

Craft knife or scalpel

Pigment binder and pigments or fabric paints in various colors

Two 5 cm (2 in) household paintbrushes

Saucers

A damp cloth

Sponge

Iron

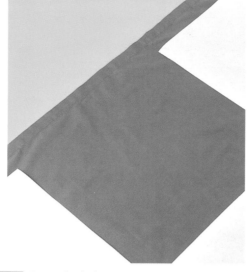

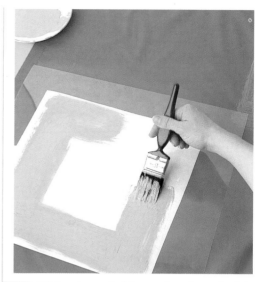

1 Lay a bed sheet out on a flat surface. Mark out the checkered pattern you will print by cutting 30 cm (12 in) square pieces of paper and laying them out on the sheet. Cut three pieces of acetate (one for each color) approximately 40 cm (16 in) square. This allows extra acetate to make a border for the area we will be printing.

2 With a household paintbrush apply fabric paint quite roughly on to a square of acetate. It is worth experimenting on a scrap piece of fabric before attempting to print on to the sheet. This will help you gauge how much paint will be required.

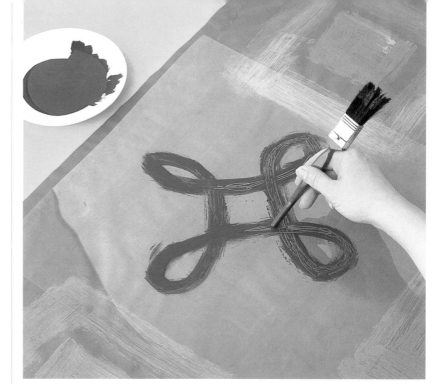

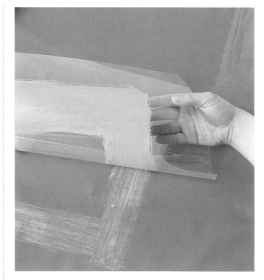

3 Place the painted side of the acetate on to the fabric. Rub the back of the acetate with your hand, and peel away to reveal your brush marks. Allow each square of color to dry before printing the next alternate square. Imagine doing only the black squares on a chess board. Once dry, finish the remaining squares.

4 The same technique can be used to paint more figurative elements (see page 125). Simply paint your shape on to the acetate, the simpler the shape, the more dramatic the final result. If you make a mistake, wipe the acetate clean with a damp cloth and start again. Once you are happy with the painted shape, scratch into the wet paint with the end of the brush to give more texture. Apply to the fabric as before.

5 Another way to produce printed shapes on fabric is to use a sponge, the sort you might wash your car with. With a marker pen draw your shape, then cut it out with a scalpel. Dip the sponge into paint and print straight on to the fabric.

6 You can see how I have continued to overprint, with dashes, three leaf clovers and a larger clover leaf. Once again, paint on to the acetate and with the end of the brush scratch into the pattern. When you are happy with the image, turn the acetate over and print on to the fabric. When you have finished working, iron the back of the sheet to fix the paint before sewing the two sheets together.

CHECKERED BLIND

Sadly we are not all fortunate enough to have glorious views of a rolling landscape appearing from each window. In fact, being realistic, the majority of us will overlook or be overlooked by someone. A good solution is to deflect interest from the view outside and focus interest on to the window treatment itself.

SHOPPING LIST

PIGMENT BINDER AND PIGMENTS OR FABRIC PAINTS

4 SAUCERS TO MIX THE PAINT IN

TWO 5 CM (2 IN) HOUSEHOLD PAINTBRUSHES

ACETATE

A PLAIN BLIND

LOW-TACK TAPE

RULER/TAPE MEASURE

1 I mixed four similar colors of fabric paints, ranging from an orange yellow to a strong red, which will all sit comfortably together on the blind. Paint large brush strokes in the lightest color with the household brush onto a sheet of acetate.

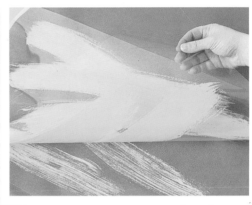

2 Place the painted acetate face down on the blind. Rub the back with your hand, and peel it away. Repeat the process until the blind is lightly covered with the first color. Leaving each color to dry before continuing with the next, continue until each of the four shades has been applied

3 Once you have covered the background of the blind with color, measure and mark out evenly spaced, large stripes going across the blind with low-tack tape. Paint in the stripes with one of the colors from the back-ground, using a household paintbrush. I did not want to make this a solid color so I have been sparing with the paint and scrubbed it into the blind leaving small areas of texture showing through. Leave to dry.

4 Repeat the process, painting the vertical stripes down the blind with another color from the background. Leave to dry flat.

TIP

A light-proof blind is best for this project as light coming through will spoil the design.

This is not the time-consuming mosaic that intricate Roman pavements are made up of; this is much easier. It is also completely addictive and lots of fun. If you have never tried this before then start with the kitchen pots (page 103), small and oh-so-simple, and work up to the garden table (page 115), which is not really any more difficult, just larger.

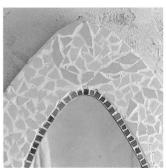

MAKING
MOSAIC

MOSAIC KITCHEN POTS

Apart from my kettle, these mosaic pots are the
most treasured posessions in my kitchen.
They have filled a bare corner with color and provide
a real contrast with their surroundings.

They really do take no time or expertise to achieve,
in fact I would suggest you may want to
have a few extra pots around when you start as you
will find it hard to stop. Before you know it
you will have a family of mosaic pots and bowls of all
shapes and sizes in your collection.

SHOPPING LIST

MOSAIC TILES

CRAFT KNIFE OR SCALPEL

TERRACOTA POTS WITH UNGLAZED EXTERIORS

TILE GROUT

TILE CUTTERS

CLOTH

BOWL OF WARM WATER

1 Mosaic tiles are bought in 30 cm (12 in) square sheets with a paper backing protecting the face of each tile. Cut these into strips that are long enough to go around the pot

2 Decide upon the order of the different colored tiles. Cover the pot with grout and start to lay the strips of tiles in position.

3 With tile cutters, cut some tiles in half and then into quarters.

4 Grout the lip of the jar and stick quarter tiles around it. Repeat the process on the lid of the jar.

104

5 Check the grout is dry, then with a cloth and some warm water dampen the paper backing and leave it for a few minutes to soak up the water, unfortunately you cannot rush this bit. Peel away the paper and wipe over the tiles with a cloth and clean water to remove any gum.

6 Finally grout the whole pot and lid to fill any gaps. Wipe away any excess grout with a damp cloth.

BASIN SPLASHBACK

The subject of preventing water from splashing our walls can, quite honestly, be rather dull. Unfortunately we have to be practical about these matters. However it is attention to detail that makes all the difference and this handsome splashback, which took such a short time to make, really adds a finishing touch to my newly decorated bathroom.

SHOPPING LIST

- TAPE MEASURE/RULER
- MARKER PEN
- MARINE PLYWOOD BOARD
- JIGSAW OR FRETSAW
- SANDPAPER
- TILE CUTTERS
- MOSAIC TILES
- 2.5 CM (1 IN) HOUSEHOLD PAINTBRUSH
- PVA GLUE
- WATERPROOF GROUT
- SPONGE
- WARM WATER
- DRY CLOTH

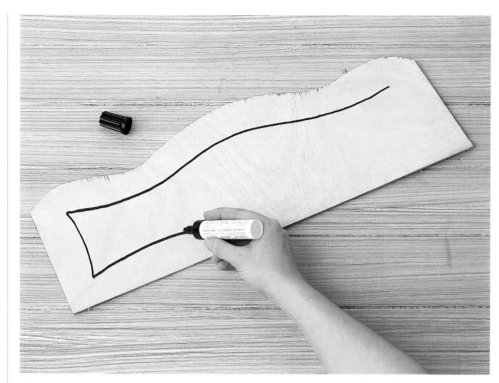

1 Start by measuring the width of basin and the height of the taps. With these measurements in mind, work out the shape of the splashback. Draw out the design on to the board with a marker pen, then cut out the shape with a jigsaw or fretsaw. Sand the edges.

TIPS

Use marine plywood and waterproof grout so that the splashback is completely practical and waterproof.

2 With tile cutters cut all the mosaic tiles into quarters.

3 Work on one area of the splashback at a time. Cover an area with a thick layer of undiluted PVA glue and place each tile in position.

4 Once you have covered the whole splashback with tiles, leave it to dry overnight. Once dry, soak off the backing paper. Cover it with grout and while the grout remains moist wipe away any excess with a dry cloth.

MOSAIC MIRROR

I love this project because it looks complicated and expensive, but, although I am sorry to disappoint you, it is neither of these! Decide upon the shape you want: circular, oval, square or break with convention and try a jigsaw-piece shape.

I made this mirror to go in a bathroom that was painted yellow. However, this mirror will sit happily in any room and you can use tiles that match, complement or even clash with the surrounding colors.

SHOPPING LIST

PAPER

PENCIL

LOW-TACK TAPE

PLYWOOD

MIRROR WITH GROUND EDGES

MIRROR MASTIC

SCREWS AND A METAL PICTURE HOOK

MARKER PEN

TILE CUTTERS

FOR AN OVAL MIRROR 48 CM (19 IN) BY 77 CM (31 IN):

6 DARK YELLOW TILES

10 LIGHT YELLOW TILES

40 SMALL MOSAIC TILES IN BLUES AND TURQUOISES

PVA WOOD GLUE

GROUT

SPONGE OR RAG

TIPS

You really don't have to spend a lot of money on expensive tiles to make this mirror, I have used cheap bathroom tiles. Avoid patterned tiles as the end result can look too busy and don't use matt or unglazed terracotta tiles as the grout will stick to the surface. Other than this you can use anything at all.

1 Decide on the size and shape of your mirror and the width of the tiled border and make a paper template. Stick this to the wall with low-tack tape to give you an idea of what the finished piece will look like in your home. Draw round the template on to a piece of plywood and cut this to size. Cut out the part of the template showing the shape you want the mirror glass to be and have a piece cut to size at a glass merchants.

2 Screw the picture hook to the back of the plywood near the top. Glue the mirror to the plywood with mirror mastic. With a marker pen draw your pattern on to the plywood. With the tiles cutters start to break up the tiles into small pieces, discarding the straight sides of the tiles. Do not be too worried about the shape of each individual piece, you will be amazed how the irregular shapes fit together.

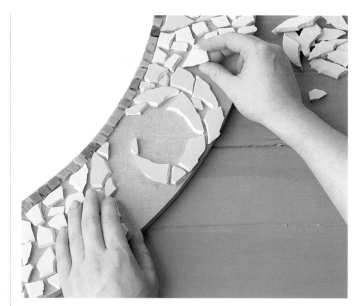

3 Start by placing the darker yellow tile pieces on to the swirl shapes. When these are in place fill in the gaps with the lighter tiles. Cut the small square tiles into quarters with the cutters and use them to border the mirror.

4 With PVA wood glue stick each tile on to the plywood. Leave to dry. Once set, grout all the gaps between the tiles and wipe the surface clean with a sponge or an old rag before leaving to it dry. You can paint the edge of the plywood with emulsion or acrylic paint to match the tiles.

MOSAIC GARDEN TABLE

There is nothing nicer than eating *alfresco* on warm summer days. However, I like to have flexibility with every piece of furniture I own so when the nights draw in, my garden table comes indoors and doubles up as a kitchen or dining table.

This mosaic table has been in constant use from the moment it was created. It seems hard to imagine how I coped without it. It has also become a real conversation piece with my friends, and I have had lots of requests to make more tables. However, I just tell them how it was done and they happily go off to make their own versions, because it really is simple.

SHOPPING LIST

TABLE

MARKER PEN

DINNER PLATE

SHEETS OF MOSAIC TILES

TILE CUTTERS

PVA GLUE

CRAFT KNIFE OR SCALPEL

WARM WATER

CLOTH

WATERPROOF GROUT

SPONGE

1 Decide where you want to place the table settings. Once you have done this, simply draw them directly on the table by tracing around a dinner plate with a marker pen.

2 To start the circle of tiles you will need to cut some of the tiles into quarters. Have a pile prepared to work with. Paint some PVA glue thickly on to the table top and start the center of the circle with the small broken tiles. Build up the pattern using whole tiles until the circle is complete. Press gently with your hands over the circle to make sure that all the tiles have made contact with the glue. Repeat this process for all the circles.

3 Now fill up the gaps. Lay the sheets of tiles on to the table, paper side up, and with a scalpel cut the backing paper around the edges of the mosaic circles and along the table's sides. Don't worry about any odd corners as they will be filled in later. Cover the surface that the tiles are going to cover with a thick layer of PVA then lay the tiles in place. Gently press down so that the glue makes contact with the tiles.

4 When you have covered all the background in sheets of tiles, leave the table overnight to make sure that the glue is really dry. With a wet cloth soak off the paper backing. Dampen it, leave it for a few minutes then effortlessly peel the backing paper away to reveal your table. To me this is the most exciting part. Suddenly all your work is uncovered and it's always a surprise.

5 Cut tiles to fit any odd corners and glue them in place. Now grout the tabletop. I have used waterproof grout because I want to use this table outside on summer evenings. Simply smooth a small amount of grout over the tiles, filling in the gaps.

6 Wipe away the excess grout with a dry cloth. Finally, with a damp sponge wipe away any smears of grout and leave to dry. You may need to repeat the grouting once the grout is dry as it can shrink away from the tiles on the first application.

VARIATIONS

You can use this technique to cover almost any flat surface with mosaic. If you are nervous about embarking on a table straight away, try doing a tray or a shelf first. This would also be an excellent technique to use to revive battered kitchen worktops, though if they are made of plastic, ensure that you use a compatible glue.

TEMPLATES

There are several ways to use the templates on these pages, either as motifs for gilding, stenciling or printing or you can use them for papercrafts, either by photocopying them or tracing them on to colored paper. You will often want to make a template into a stencil and there is a very simple way to do this. Tape the photocopy to a window with low-tack tape, then tape your stencil card over the photocopy. The light coming through the window will allow you to see through the card to the photocopied template. Trace off the template and then cut out the stencil carefully with a craft knife or scalpel on a cutting mat – no messy fussing with carbon paper or tracing paper.

**GILDED AND DÉCOUPAGED
FRUIT BOWL**
page 34
(enlarge to 140%)

GILDED GLASS TABLE
page 28
(enlarge to 140%)

CELTIC KNOT WALL TREATMENT
page 39
(enlarge to 140%)

STENCILED CUSHION COVERS
page 42
(enlarge to 140%)

STENCILED CUSHION COVERS
page 42
(enlarge to 140%)

STENCILED CUSHION COVERS
page 42
(enlarge to 140%)

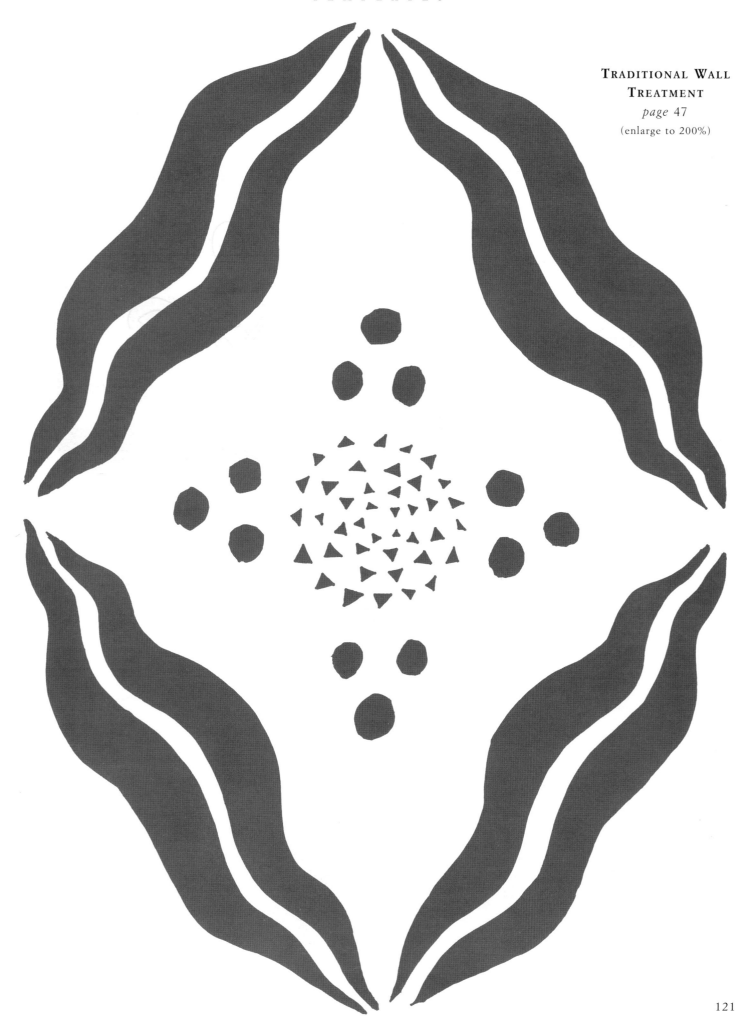

TRADITIONAL WALL
TREATMENT
page 47
(enlarge to 200%)

ANIMAL PLAYMAT
page 48
(enlarge to 140%)

ANIMAL PLAYMAT
page 48
(enlarge to 140%)

Animal Playmat
page 48
(enlarge to 140%)

SILK ROOM DIVIDER
page 87
(enlarge to 150%)

**STENCILED AND STITCHED
BLANKET**
page 56
(enlarge to 150%)

PATTERNED BED LINEN
page 94
(enlarge to 150%)

SUPPLIERS

Ocean of Notions, Inc
10990 Biscayne Boulevard,
Miami,
Florida 33161
(800-626-8410).

Factory Direct Craft Supply
315 Conover Drive,
Franklin,
Ohio 45005
(800-252-5223).

Audrias Crafts
6821 McCart,
Fort Worth,
Texas 76133
(800-433 2918).

Boleks Crafts
Post Office Box 465,
Dover,
Ohio 44622
(800-743-2723).

Treasure Island
187 Columbia Turnpike,
Florham Park,
New Jersey 07932
(800-648-0109).

New York Central Art Suppliers
62 Third Avenue,
New York,
New York 10003
(800-950-6111).

Jo-Ann Fabrics and Crafts
5381 Darrow Road,
Hudson,
Ohio 44236
(216-650-6228).

Framing, Fabrics and Molding
947 Cole Avenue,
Los Angeles,
California 90038
(800-832-2742).

Pyramid Art Supply
100 Paragon Parkway,
Mansfield,
Ohio 44903
(800-637-0955).

Pearl Paints
308 Canal Street,
New York,
New York 10013
(800-451-7327).

Art Express
1224 Lincoln Street,
Columbia,
South Carolina 29201
(800-535-5908).

ACKNOWLEDGEMENTS

To some it must appear that I and I alone have put this book together. Well, this is far from the truth, in fact none of this would have been possible without wonderful team work. Many thanks go out to all the friends and colleagues who have made this such a wonderful success.

Lucinda Symons – for your exquisite photography, for bringing this book to life with your tireless creative input and for being such a terrific laugh. This book is as much yours, and I hope very much to work with you in the future. Dearest Miranda – thanks for loads of support and encouragement just when it really counted. Vicky and Rachael – for being able to see ahead of the game. Kate Haxell – thank you for those moments of utter genius, encouraging words, and that ever-watchful gaze. Cindy Richards – for having exceptionally good taste. Roger Bristow – for creatively allowing a free rein. Janet James – for your unleashed talent in putting this book together

Love and thanks go to all those friends that play such an important part in my life. Darling Tim Killingbeck – I consider myself very fortunate to have a friend in you. John Briffa – who has inspired some of what you have read. Malcolm Hulme – for nights of endless laughter. You will always be my beloved neighbour. Emma Cherry – I have finally found my kindred spirit. Darling sister Juliet for your endless love and support. Joanne Barnet – you're as precious as a friend can get. Sally – whose generosity and love knows no bounds. Robert Atherton – for your words of wisdom. Kate and Gemma Robbins – for so kindly allowing me to borrow your toys. Finally to Mr Scholar, my English teacher, who would often say of my lengthy essays: 'I know that your stories are absolutely wonderful Andrea, the only problem is that I can't read them.' Unfortunately English and spelling were not my strong point, which makes writing for a living so amusing. Dear Mr Scholar, I'm living proof that things can get better, if you try hard enough!!!

INDEX

A

animal playmat (stenciled) 48-51

B

basin splashback, mosaic 106-109
bathrooms:
    basin splashback (mosaic) 106-109
    mosaic mirror 110-113
    papered shelf 78-79
bed linen, patterned 94-97
blanket, stenciled and stitched 56-59
blinds:
    checkered (painted) 98-99
    cutwork 80-83
bowl:
    gilded and découpaged 34-37
    see also jug; pots
brushes:
    for gilding 10
    for painting and printing 16
    for papercraft 14
    for stenciling 12

C

Celtic knot wall treatment (gilding) 38-39
checkered blind (painted) 98-99
chest of drawers, papered and gilded 70-73
curtains:
    velvet (painted) 90-93
    see also blinds
cushion covers, stenciled 42-45
cutting boards, resealing 12
cutwork blind 80-83

D

découpage:
    découpaged and pierced lampshades 66-69
    gilded and découpaged fruit bowl 34-37

diamond-patterned lampshade (gilded) 24-27

F

fabrics:
    painting and printing 16, 85
        bed linen 94-97
        checkered blind 98-99
        silk room divider 86-89
        velvet curtains 90-93
    stenciling 42-45
        animal playmat 48-51
        blanket 56-59
        cushion covers 42-45
flower pots, gilded 22-23
frames, two-colour (gilded) 32-33
frosted mirror (stenciled) 60-63
fruit bowl, gilded and découpaged 34-37
furniture:
    garden table 114-117
    gilded glass table 28-31
    papered and gilded chest of drawers 70-73

G

garden table, mosaic 114-117
gilding 10, 21
    Celtic knot wall treatment 38-39
    diamond-patterned lampshade 24-27
    galvanized metal pots 22-23
    gilded and découpaged fruit bowl 34-37
    glass table 28-31
    papered and gilded chest of drawers 70-73
    two-colour picture frames 32-33
glass:
    gilded glass table 28-31
    gilded two-colour picture frames 32-33

mirrors:
    frosted stenciled 60-63
    mosaic bathroom 110-113
    papered bathroom shelf 78-79
glue, PVA 14
grouting 18, 109, 113, 117

J

jug, plaid (stenciled) 52-55

K

kitchen pots, mosaic 102-105

L

lampshades:
    découpaged and pierced 66-69
    diamond-patterned (gilded) 24-27
layout paper 14
leaf, metal 10
    applying *see* gilding

M

mat *see* playmat
metal leaf 10
    applying *see* gilding
metallic paints 16
mirrors:
    bathroom (mosaic) 110-113
    frosted (stenciled) 60-63
mosaics 18, 101
    basin splashback 106-109
    bathroom mirror 110-113
    garden table 114-117
    kitchen pots 102-105

P

painting and printing 16, 85
    bed linen 94-97
    checkered blind 98-99
    silk room divider 86-89
    velvet curtains 90-93

paints:
  concentrated colour pigment 16
  for stenciling 12
  metallic 16
paper:
  layout 14
  photocopying 14
  watercolour 14
papercrafts 14, 65
  bathroom shelf 78-79
  cutwork blind 80-83
  découpaged and pierced
    lampshades 66-69
  gilded and découpaged fruit bowl
    34-37
  papered and gilded chest of
    drawers 70-73
  screen 74-77
photocopying paper 14
picture frames, two-colour (gilded)
  32-33
pierced lampshades 66-69
plaid jug (stenciled) 52-55

playmat, stenciled 48-51
pots:
  gilded 22-23
  kitchen (mosaic) 102-105
  see also bowl; jug
printing *see* painting and printing
PVA glue 14

room dividers:
  paper 74-77
  silk (painted) 86-89

screens:
  paper 74-77
  silk room divider (painted) 86-89
shades *see* lampshades
shelf, bathroom (papered) 78-79
silk room divider (painted) 86-89
size 10
splashback, mosaic 106-109
sponge printing 97

stencil brushes 12
stenciling 12, 41
  animal playmat 48-51
  blanket 56-59
  Celtic knot wall treatment (gilding)
    38-39
  cushion covers 42-45
  frosted mirror 60-63
  plaid jug 52-55
  traditional wall treatment 46-47

tables:
  garden (mosaic) 114-117
  gilded glass 28-31
tiles, mosaic 18
  see mosaics

wall treatments, stenciled:
  gilded Celtic knot 38-39
  traditional 46-47
watercolor paper 14